Ol' Brown Eyes Is Back

Jennifer Juan

Contents

About This Book

Jennifer Juan's poetry collection, Ol' Brown Eyes Is Back is a triumphant cry of freedom, and an emancipation from the old insecurities and ideals that so many find themselves trapped by.

Filled with honest, healing verses that tell a story of self discovery, healing and the road to self acceptance, Ol' Brown Eyes Is Back is witty but heartfelt, giving fresh perspectives on millennial life, the perils of romance, mental health and the modern world, finding beauty in life's hardest moments, and celebrating the joy in the finest.

For everyone travelling through life who needs to hear that they're not alone, this volume will be a breath of fresh air and a comforting friend, for the good times and the bad.

For the girl who decided to live, and the people who made that decision easier x

__Composition__

I stopped reading about myself,
and finally slept,
alone in the dark.
Is this growing up?
Glowing up?
Will I finally be,
the girl,
I dreamed I could,
or the woman,
clinging to a girl that feels safe?

I'll live my life on the internet.
Snapchat smiles,
digital diamonds,
releasing records,
about the boys and girls I can't forget.
I'll be the hero,
in the novel I know I won't finish.
I'll be the coolest girl you've never met.

Piano loops,
rain sounds,

from the speakers,
the one window I could afford,
in the city I inherited.
It is night,
and the days to come haunt me.

Sant Jordi

We pretend that we aren't swayed,

but we still stay in awe of the twenty four hour magic,

the way everybody smiles just a little bit more,

the electric in our fingertips,

as we hold hands,

(just in case we get lost, definitely NOT because we
are in love),

we go about the day,

slightly sailing through the air.

You gave me a single crimson rose,

while I signed my soul into seventy seven books,

ignoring you,

from my book fair booth,

but still looking up every few seconds,

to check you were still cutting back in line,

to get my attention,

with your single crimson rose.

You are a waste of my time,

and a waste of my words,

or so I told myself,

as I signed my last book,

making it out to the waste I loved most in the world,

I singed my soul,

in black ink,

branded on the book I wish I didn't write about you.

As night fell,

the day dancing down the street,

and out of sight,

you were still in line, all alone,

with your single crimson red rose,

not seeming to understand why it wasn't enough,

for a girl who gave a gift,

that would last forever.

You held the sharp stem in your hands,

so tightly that you bled,

crawling onto the table of the booth,

under the soft, spring moon,

to declare to the town,

(that didn't really care),

that you would grow me a garden of roses,

if I would stay and watch you grow.

I watered you,
from my eyes.

A Passion That Had Moved Into His Body, Like A Stranger

I see you,
when I fall asleep...

I dream of our days,
smoking stolen, scolding cigarettes,
misbehaving in meadows,
convincing myself I won't miss you,
when we inevitably part,
listening to Crispin Glover albums,
pretending I understand,
some secret meaning,
in every song,
because it makes me feel smart,
and I forget,
how intimidated I am,
by your degree,
and your height.

but in my dreams,
you're out of reach...

Lured into a trap,

by a trail of fruit salad chewits,

and tulips,

I stare up at you,

the cutest kidnapper in the wilds of west Kent,

as you pick me up,

romantic and rugged,

taking me back to your lair.

and I take my pills now,

you learn to breathe...

I glide across your bedroom carpet,

broken vacuum,

taking nothing from your world,

but making more noise than you ever imagined,

kept around,

because you're a heart hungry hoarder,

monumentally sentimental,

and maybe that's why she left you,

and maybe that's why I will never leave,

even when I am on the other end of Europe.

you dream of me,

we're who we need to see...

I dream of our days,
after all this time,
all the time,
streaming Clowny Clown Clown,
reading that last letter you sent,
hoping my new kidnapper doesn't hear me cry.

and I see you,
when I fall asleep...

Super Snow Moon

Sitting under the super snow moon,
with you,
sneaking glances and kisses,
whispering our wishes,
in case the stars can hear our secrets,
fingers intertwined,
as I lean into your embrace,
wondering how long I can hope to have you,
and if this is what the world meant,
when they said that love was magic.

Do Babies Know That Life Is A Scam?

There is a baby staring at me,
and I have to wonder,
if she dreams as big as I used to do.
I used to dream,
in narcotic neon,
of the things the world could be,
but now,
all I have left,
is the hope that she still can,
before she has to face up to the harrowing horrors of
2019.

Or,
maybe she's just a baby,
who looks at stuff,
because that's what babies do,
and I'm still losing my mind,
despite me telling everyone I'm fine,
because that's what millennials do.

Driving In Circles

We are in the car.

You are so incensed

by my obscene suggestion,

that your affection for me,

makes you an Anglophile,

that you have forgotten how car sick you normally
get.

We are in the car.

I am so obsessed,

with the way the sun always seems to be present
when you are,

shining against your eyes,

the warmest shade of brown,

it becomes hard to forget how much I want to kiss
you.

We are in the car.

We are so late for dinner,

but it doesn't seem to matter,

because we have your emergency stash of
shortbread,

and we have each other,

to kiss,

or to cannibalise.

We forget about dinner,

pulling over,

enjoying each other,

under the embarrassed eyes,

of the ever present sun.

Foster Parents

You always come home,
with flowers that you fostered,
but we're bad parents.

The Girl On The Island

To answer the question,
I asked the shore,
unsure and afraid,
on all the summer days,
I spent,
breathing at the bottom of the ocean,
so the hands that craved the chance to save me,
could not reach me.

Yes.

To the boy on the island,
who gave the city to a country girl,
in one cataclysmic kiss.
Who watched the girl ask,
again and again,
something he already knew,
reaching down into the rains around them,
no matter how many times she fell,
pulling her to safe dryness.

Yes.

Yes,
I am enough.
Yes,
we're in love.

<u>Crying Crayons</u>

The days are grey,
and I'm blue for you,
but I'm dropping the recipe for a rainbow,
from my brown eyes.

Here's To The Kids Who Wear Purple

You taught me to love,
showing me how to put familiar fondness
in the single fondant fancy I would find,
hiding in my lunch box,
alongside salad sandwiches,
that tasted of
"Have a good day."
"Come home safe."
"You are the thing I have loved most,
in this wild, wide world."

I watched you wash my clothes,
turning them from fashion to compassion,
sending me into the world each day,
wrapped in wishes that I would be wise and well,
sending me to sleep,
with stories,
soft pyjamas,
and a small night light made of the stars from the sky,
you always taught me was mine to aim for.

So,

why,

when I loved someone,

who loved me too,

the way you taught me,

with kindness,

selflessly,

more than I had ever loved anyone,

in this wild, wide world,

did you suddenly stop?

Hitchcock In A Push Up Bra

We can kiss

and touch

and forget the proper way of using connectives,

existing,

in a beautiful reverie,

where nobody can hurt us,

and you,

will be fascinated by me,

because I tell you too,

and we are just in my head,

living out the movies I direct,

every time I see you.

Yes. No. Yes. No.

Yes,

I was so dramatic,

but that's what you loved about me,

I was a tempest,

a teen temptress,

slamming doors,

stirring you up,

tearing the whole room apart,

until you could take no more,

kissing away my kicking and screaming.

No,

I didn't have a clue,

and there are things that nobody can teach you,

until you are ready to be taught.

I dreamed at dusk,

turning to Taylor and Adele,

to try and figure out why you were so cruel,

to someone who lived so passionately for you.

Yes,

your efforts to protect me,

from the violence of your disturbing desire,

felt cruel,

because all I knew,

was how to want you.

I toiled in time,

that wasn't spent in a smitten storm,

that raged all around you,

possessively pouring,

never quite catching you,

because you had selfishly decided,

that you were staying inside,

to wait out the vengeful weather,

that you had spent many nights praying for.

No,

I suppose you didn't think it through,

when you were gazing out,

at the fruitless fields,

that you thought had flowered for the last time.

I suppose you didn't think it through,

as you sat at your desk,

leaving lupins for Mother Nature,

and asking her,

for fresh,

young spring rain.

Oh, Mate

How can you call yourself a grown man,
a good man,
taller than the trees man,
be there when I need you man,
the one I can trust man,
making me laugh man,
here for the right reasons man,
not being a prick, man,
not after one thing man,
take me out for coffee and a catch up man,
text me just to see how I am man,
allegedly a grown, good man.

How can you call yourself a grown man,
when your childish arse still believes in the friend
zone?
At your age, man?
Asking me for things you never ask of your male
friends man,
acting like all my girl friends man,
but still thinking it means something different for a
man,
man?

Oh, _**mate**_.

Everyone's Tough Until Franceska Mann Comes Around

Bright lights,

impossibly shined through days of darkness,

as you began your last show.

Sunday's child,

happy and wise,

each soft step,

echoed from the orchestra,

to the chambers,

as you pulled red curtains,

from his chest,

applause shooting from their guns.

You spin,

a signal,

swans swarm the crowd,

scalping,

saving,

swinging to the song you left behind.

Everyone's tough,

until Ms Mann comes around.

Indeed I Do

It doesn't matter,
where in the world I venture,
how many names I perfectly print,
before scribbling out,
until the page is as black as the night.
I will always find my way back to you,
because your name is written
on every inch of my soul,
and I am a seasick sweetheart,
saying the same six letters,
until my throat is sore and smiling.
Repeat.
Repeat.
Repeat.
Repeat.

The Trouble With Moving To Los Angeles

She said she loved the scent of the stars,
that fell into her lap,
as she ascended to the air.
The world belonged to her,
looking luxurious,
from so high up,
and it was beautiful,
like the pictures in the books she'd borrowed,
from the lonely library,
of the ghost town she had been risen from,
an overzealous zombie,
with ideas too big for the place.

Yes,
it was beautiful,
like the girls she saw,
at the coffee shop,
and the endless spin classes,
pretty dolls,
never too tall,
or too small,
with green smoothies,

heavenly bodies,

that left her green with envy,

until she remembered she was in Hollyweird,

and she could play any role she wanted.

Yes,

it was beautiful.

The world was beautiful.

The girls were beautiful.

Her friends were beautiful.

Her home was beautiful.

Her hair was beautiful.

Her dreams were beautiful.

Her drugs were beautiful.

Her loves were beautiful.

Her bank balance was beautiful.

Her life was beautiful.

Just all so beautiful,

until life began to crawl up the clouds,

and into her lap,

crushing the stars,

clawing at her hair,

ascending her extensions,

to confront her.

She said she wanted it all,
until she had it,
but don't we all?

Nothing Really Matters

Three thousand,
two hundred,
and,
eighty two days,
had passed.
I had a cold,
like the night we met,
but for the very first time,
sniffling and scarred,
I forgot your name.

I fell,
free,
a supersonic woman,
into the cinema seat.
I fell in love,
once again,
with Freddy Mercury,
because he didn't belong to you,
any longer,
and,
for the first time,

since I left you,
neither did I.

Bunny Rabbit

Giving you the night sweats,
teasing you to terror.
Would you like it,
if I accommodated your affection,
darling?
Do you like the delights
of our velvet nights?
Burning with desire,
for your bunny rabbit,
like a wealthy, deviant alcoholic,
you think me into your throat,
shaking so,
as I go down,
drinking yourself to death.
The thrill tastes too good to resist.
Devout,
to the point of disturbing,
waiting and writhing,
sighing and yearning.

It's A Prank, Bro

People say I'm so loud,
but they never hear me.
I spend several hours,
every day,
screaming in every language I know,
including basic Klingon,
about the scars of off hand remarks,
the way expectations follow me around,
and sit,
across from me,
smirking as I continue to scream,
and scream,
until my throat checks out,
and heads to the hospital.

She described me once,
in a letter to my father,
as bubbly.
The bubbles are on the stove.
I have boiled,
and boiled,
and burned,

until I am a charred morsel,

morose at the bottom of a pan,

still screaming,

still trying to boil,

so bubbly it burns.

I'm convinced,

that I have an evil twin,

who visits everyone I know,

every day,

and says,

"Ignore everything I say from now on,

it's a prank, bro."

Either that,

or the people that loved me,

loved so hard,

when I was young,

loud and clear enough to hear,

loved so hard,

that they have been replaced,

by robots.

Rad But Sad

Let's teach our tears,
to change the world,
sweet resurrections,
revolutions,
a reunion,
of our souls,
and our smiles.

You know,
I'm radical,
but sad(ical),
it's all that I know how to do.
Maybe I could learn to smile,
with you,
and it will be the most radical thing,
this sad girl ever did.

Holbeck

You mistook my weakness
for kindness,
but after all this time,
I can't find it in me,
to be sweet,
and meek.
Why is it me?
Why do I wake up,
in hell every afternoon?
Maybe there is a lot more to me,
than there is to me?
You stroke my sallow cheeks,
passing me breakfast,
crack cocaine,
that I cannot stand,
but need to stand.

As I finally find my feet,
pushing last night under the sofa,
with the ash tray,
I glance at the grey, grubby glass,
of the window,

paralysed by the memory,
of the way you throw me to the pack,
counting their money as they grab me.
I glance,
eyes glazed,
wondering if I could see my freedom,
for a moment,
before the sun sets,
and the lights turn red.
I'll be kind,
tonight,
if you want me to.

Beautiful Bad Hombre

You'll figure it out someday,

striking the glass of a million dreams,

with the atrociously adorable face you possess,

my luscious lost boy,

beautiful bad hombre,

born to lose,

losing his mind,

as he tries to learn to live.

I wear your heart on my sleeve,

and your tears on my lips.

So, You've Decided You Want To Be A Ghost

You got engaged,
to a beautiful girl,
but then you tried to kill yourself.
Life will never be able,
to satisfy those of us,
who were born drowning.
Aqua angels,
who fell to Earth,
feeling like we were never quite here,
but knowing we couldn't leave.

You came to my house.
We didn't talk about it.
I watched my girlfriend talking about me,
to the friends she has,
who say she looks at me,
like she did her dead girlfriend,
that she never got the chance to marry,
and suddenly,
(no offence)
your problems don't seem so big to me,
because I'm a ghost,

and I watched myself walk through the open door,

that I let you walk into,

sitting down with a stranger,

because,

that's the way she likes it.

I know her friends didn't mean anything by it,

and I know she probably can't help it,

and maybe someday,

she will love me for more than my long black hair,

that looks like the ghost,

she gave her heart to before.

Maybe she could learn to love something other than,

my horrible habit of smoking as I write,

death between my lips,

as I pull her into my lap,

reading back all the things,

her poltergeist princess told her years ago.

I'm sorry,

we were talking about you,

and as ghosts often do,

I disappeared into the past.

Back to you,

in the studio.

We aren't even really friends.

We're just babies who survived the same bad shit,

finding each other when life feels too hard,

and,

I guess if you want to talk,

we can talk,

but I don't know what a ghost can say,

to the boy looking at the brochure.

Make Nuclear Love, Not Nuclear War

We were the only ones left,
your left hand trembled,
on my leg,
as silence rang out,
and I counted
each shard of glass,
that had captured the carpet.
The bombs had come to visit,
my love,
and somehow,
we survived.

You carried me,
carefully,
across the river of window.
We ran outside,
like children,
at playtime,
holding hands,
in case we got lost,
in a world that belonged to us.

It was bland,

and brown,

but I still thought it was beautiful,

like the same pasta and pesto,

you made me,

before,

and after the apocalypse,

because I didn't know how to be adventurous.

Being with you,

under the beating sun,

that seemed to stay forever,

as we walked the empty streets,

made me forget,

that everyone,

and everything,

we had loved,

was lost,

and my heart,

beat,

humbled and hurried,

only for you.

Surfer Moon

Remaining forevermore,
pining for the past,
so lucky to be lovesick,
living my whole life,
for that Saturday,
waiting by the waves for you,
dancing under the surfer moon,
to the crashing cymbals of the sea.

Please don't put my heart in the hands,
of your rock and roll band.

I remember
when it wasn't so hard to love you,
the hopeful hems of my summer dresses,
holding on to your hands,
never daring to think,
that your hands would abandon them,
or me,
leaving me waiting,
as the waves rush home,
and the surfer moon rides away.

Tea With Theresa

The heir apparent.
The dashing deputy.
Beauty on a billboard,
posters pasted over blood splatters.

It doesn't matter,
women can drive now!

The blood pools from many different places,
including the veins of his own land.
Theresa May is a feminist.
THIS
IS
WHAT
A
FEMINIST
LOOKS
LIKE
She holds the hands of a million men,
who wound women (and children, and men).
Jeremy Hunt says we have shared values,
and Prince Charles will dance for them,

so the children,

the journalists,

the activists can laugh one last time,

before they leave with the parting sun.

Fifty thousand Yemeni children,

starved to death,

in 2017,

but we are starving,

to sell their killer fighter jets,

because everyone knows,

death feels divine,

when the last thing you see is the Union Jack.

Tell your boss, the deed was done.

Lilac Lighter

Lilac lighter lays,
on the table,
where I trembled under your touch,
telling you your own name,
on repeat,
like a scratched, sensual CD.

You couldn't sleep,
smiling through insomnia,
staring down at the table,
clicking the lilac lighter,
on repeat,
trying to make an inferno,
as dangerous and delicious as that night.

Arts and Crafts

From seven to seven,

I walk the streets,

sewing each sobbing section of myself back together,

even though I know,

the second I walk through the door,

you will unpick every stitch,

until I am a forlorn fountain of fabric,

falling,

with traumatic elegance,

in a pile,

by the unwelcoming welcome mat.

Early Autumn

Walls explode around us,
terror tears tarnished paint,
impossible, defiant futures,
trampling on loneliness.

We are peroxide,
burning through the dullest days,
blinding mirrors,
raising rainbows to wrap ourselves in.

We dream of death,
sleeping souls, surrounded by green leaves,
too young to have fallen,
but hungry to be close to us.

You are locked inside a salmon shirt.
I long to set you free,
begging my shaking hands,
to cooperate.

Hazel Gaze

There is home,
in your hazel gaze.
Don't you know?
I tell you every day.
I come up with some new, pretentious way,
to let you know,
that my eyes grow real wide,
and my mouth gets real slow,
when I see you,
and your hazel gaze.

Lately,
I spend my days,
as always,
waiting to hear your laugh,
so rare,
refined,
reserved for when I am at my most awkward.
Oh,
the truth is,
I spend my days,
in delusional dazes,

picking you daisies,
that despite your acceptance
of my innocent ineptitude towards romance,
I remain to shy to show you.

So,
I stay sat,
imagining your embrace,
wrapped up in smoke,
that is no substitute,
for the warmth of the way,
you pull me from my books,
because I forgot to eat,
watching over me,
with that hazel gaze,
and all your witchy, wicked ways,
that charmed a helpless, hapless honey,
to give over her mind,
and a key to her flat.

I was so busy,
laying in luxury loneliness,
writing yet another poem,
about you,

and that...
Darling,
I'm going to say it again.
Dazing,
hazel,
gaze,
as always,
but you aren't here,
to remind me,
that I cannot exist on dreams alone,
so,
I suppose I'll starve to death.

Unless,
you want to come over?

Spirits

I thought I was okay,
walking on air,
and adventure,
through a house that is big enough,
to accommodate my ambition and my issues,
waving at the way I was,
collected clingy calls,
on restless needy nights,
that feel a lifetime away,
because I have built a better beauty,
who enjoys the echoes of an empty home,
and I have forgotten to feel some type of way,
when I scroll past you,
on my Facebook feed.
It totally works.
See?
I'm not thinking about you at all,
and I don't...
Wait.
Oh no.
Suddenly,
I am swarmed with spirits,

and the nights feel needy,
and restless again.
I'm haunted,
hanging out at my home made bar,
languishing liquor,
licking away at the loneliness,
but I still taste your name,
in every sip of spirits.

MySpace

Sitting in the dark,
because the light offends your sensibilities.
You say you're washed up,
sarcastically,
while unloading the dishwasher.
You see your dreams,
dancing down the drain,
as you pass the sink,
throwing your best china,
out into the garden.
You frightened off the birds,
and they were your only audience,
these days.

Living in la la land,
laughing when the landlord sends another letter.
You dance around the kitchen,
to keep you warm,
when the gas company cuts you off.
You finally realise that you can't eat dreams,
and a wish won't pay the rent.
I watch you,

from the future,

that you never could reach,

thinking of the way you use to sing and dance for me.

Sometimes I miss you,

so I take a seat,

where the birds used to gape at your glittery gore,

and I watch you update your MySpace.

Scavenger Hunt

I used to think I had a type,
but I'm starting to think,
in between listening to self help subliminals,
and typing up all my adventures,
that each achingly amorous affair,
was a clue,
on a scavenger hunt.

My first clue,
was a severed,
severe hand,
clutching a ruler.
I took him home,
holding him,
instead of doing my homework,
until he snaked up around my shoulders,
whispering,
"Do some bloody writing."
He rapped my knuckles,
before he bid me good day,
and stormed from the scene.

I thought of the handsome hand constantly,
until,
by chance,
on a blustery, blue Sunday,
I was swept into the sky,
until I found a cuddly cloud,
gentle and genuine,
who settled me down,
tucking me into the serene sunset.
She kissed my cheeks,
and bruised knuckles.
until I dozed into delirious dreams.

Then it began to rain.
I sank from the sky,
floating to the floor,
melting in the madness,
like a wonderful witch,
until I landed in the lap of love.

And then,
darling,
there is you.
My treasure,

that I keep buried in my bed,
under the covers,
so that I will always have balance.

The Never Ending Sacrifice

I'm talking to myself,
like I'm somebody else...

I remember dressing as a different girl each day,
because you said you loved me,
but you didn't download me as I was,
preferring to project endless expansion packs
onto my frightened form.

I have been each girl,
on your grimy,
gory screen,
playing your pet virgin,
so well,
that I look into the mirror,
and it looks just like your laptop.

Despite insisting that you love me,
you just aimed a stream of white lightning,
at my tear stained face.

Kiss me,

and I cry...

Pink Elephants

I've got nothing much to say to you,

but I'm still opening my mouth,

as pink elephants fly out.

I still love you.

I like your shirt today.

I still want you.

Maybe we should get new curtains.

I can't lose you.

It's okay if she's there,

just don't tell me.

I've got nothing much to say,

so I'll say whatever comes to mind,

to keep you mine,

for a little longer.

Donna's Date

Just seventeen,
his dreams were so tall,
eyes shining,
like the buttons he spent the morning polishing,
to make a good impression.
He dreams,
like he sings,
sweet and high,
true love on the airwaves,
young enough to believe,
that high school heaven lasts forever.

Real life is tough,
darling,
you grow up,
and you can't believe so hard,
because life is heavy,
hateful,
but his dreams are still as bright,
as the day he was born.
I watch the sky sometimes,
his voice in my ear,

his soul in my eyes,
wondering if he could have dreamed so big,
if he didn't stay so small.

<u>Gloss</u>

The fact is,

you're so matter of fact,

when you tell me that,

we're seeing each other,

one last time,

to say goodbye,

the only way we can,

to make it stick,

and I will stick to your skin,

like the glitter on my glossy lips,

this one last time,

and always.

Dear Ashli

Dear Ashli,
Do you remember the fields,
behind the school,
where you'd sit,
writing increasingly absurd verses,
about increasingly inappropriate ideas,
with nature in your knotted hair,
petals,
picked from the ground,
as if you were a girl,
in a music video of some acoustic ballad,
that you listened to on repeat,
because your Aquarius nature needed validation for
how deep you were?

That was a long question.
You do that,
and some might think it's messy,
or confusing,
but I cry at your questions,
you curious, cautious crybaby.

You always had to know,

even when it hurt,

and it almost always did,

because,

sometimes,

you're a stupid bitch,

longing for a life that is nothing but pain,

because you've seen too many movies,

and you're full of rural boredom.

One day,

you will learn that there can be just as much
excitement,

in experiencing sheer boredom,

with the right person,

than all the movie scenes that play out in your pretty
head,

which will be a relief,

after so much drama.

I'm going to be honest,

it's going to take a while,

because,

surprise!

You're very traumatised!

Interestingly enough,

years of projectile problematic passion does in fact take its toll,

and you will spend several years,

locked in a lair of loneliness and lollipops,

before you finally find the courage to venture outside,

to fetch the morning paper,

and,

I suppose,

that's where you'll find this letter,

and maybe something else that finally fulfils you.

Car Parks

There was red and blue,
in the air,
sirens singing,
as I stared up at you,
like you were an old friend,
an old memory,
a stabilising slap to the face,
among the chaotic commuters,
questioning officers,
about how they should get home,
and what they should do.

I had been worrying
about a press release,
getting to the cinema on time,
paying the council tax,
but then,
there you were,
staring down at me,
caught on the edge of the worst of life.

Caught at the edge of today,

crawling across the concrete of the car park,

your weary arms are waiting,

done with holding you up,

for all the world to see,

saying

"I still want to stay"

I watch them cling to the concrete,

whispering

"But I don't know if I can"

and I wish,

so hard,

that I could change your mind,

even though I don't know you like that,

or, at all,

actually.

I saw you live,

though,

led back from the edge of goodbye,

into the horizon,

towards help and hope,

as I,

and all the chaotic commuters cleared the road,

going back to little problems,

like press releases,

cinema dates,

council tax,

so we didn't have to think of giant concrete car parks,

and their habit of stealing people,

to take them to the sky.

Some Next Man's Other Woman

They asked you one more time,
to be stronger than the demons that stole you,
because nobody is going to save you,
sweetheart,
beyond begging you to be here one more time,
even if they won't give you a reason to stay.

They stole your heart,
dragging it from your chest,
and up your throat,
though it begged to be with you,
because there was no greater love,
but,
there was money to be made,
from your separation and desperation.

They started writing your last goodbye,
on the back of the betrayals they walked you into,
rehearsing your funeral before you even died,
couldn't love you when they had a chance,
making you the media's greatest masterpiece,
blinded by your tears in Belgrade,

begging for your beautiful broken heart to be laid to
rest beside you.

They kept your heart,

in a glass box,

surrounded by gold records.

Westminster Fields

I took my sad girl playlist,
and my delightful delusions,
down to the river,
waiting and wishing, wistfully,
for you to rise from the water,
your eyes ablaze,
your arms calling to me,
but,
as I reached the end of the playlist,
and the day drew to a close,
I knew my hopes had been held under the beautiful
bubbles,
choked,
by the text I sent,
asking you to stay away.

Of course,
you obeyed,
because you were the only bad boy
who was good to me.
That night,
I gave my heart to the valleys,
because I knew it wasn't safe with me,

and for a second,

I thought I'd give the rest of me too,

becoming the soulmate of the sky,

to keep myself,

from running back to you,

again.

Needs

There is nothing wrong with him.
Not in the sense that society expects.
He has a good job,
working with the hands that he's obsessed with,
(he always seems to talk about them,
and their alleged talents),
he's got his driving licence,
a real one,
not one of the little plastic ones,
from Legoland.

Yes,
he's a grown man.
He tells me,
all about wanting to get to know me,
but he broke into my study,
taking all my children from the shelf,
committing crime after crime,
breaking my heart,
before he had even won it,
desecrating all the days I held close
tearing down the tales I had built,

from the matter of my brain,

and the things that really mattered to me,

(which he never bothered to ask about,

by the way),

because he says my work "does it" for him,

(whatever that means)

and though I know,

it is no longer mine,

when I set it free,

it is still like watching my child,

being chased,

into the woods,

by wayward wolves,

who could never have the best of intentions.

I finally understand,

why my mother would hold my hand,

a little tighter,

when I was a girl,

as we walked past pubs,

with smoking areas,

sexual harassment minefields,

That baby is mine,

growing from my mind,

but still,

just as real and essential to me,

as if she crawled from my canal,

to arrive in my arms,

and though he thinks he's done nothing wrong,

and I am too conditioned by alleged feminine empowerment,

that always seems to centre men,

to "kink shame" him,

or prioritise my own comfort,

I feel sick,

when he tells me that he wants to fuck my baby.

He says he likes our conversations,

but they are scripted exchanges,

where I am only permitted to tell him that I'm fine,

and to act impressed

that he expresses an interest in performing oral sex on a woman,

because if I ask him to ask about my interests,

I am being boring.

If I ask him to try a little harder to make me feel special,

I am being unreasonable.

If I ask him to treat my work with the same respect I

do his,

I am being oversensitive.

If I ask him to leave me alone,

I am a bitch,

who isn't giving him a chance,

because she's up herself,

or thinks she is better than him,

because she went to university,

and does some artsy job,

and reads the papers,

or...

I know he has needs,

but so do I,

and I'm trying to find an acceptable way,

to say that he just isn't capable of fulfilling them.

Priceless

I'm sort of sentimental,
lying amongst the linen,
with a tiara I borrowed,
on top of my tresses.
Darling,
I am the quarantined Queen of Fortnum's,
locked away from everyone but you,
making mischief with two wedding day Barbies.

Borrowing make up,
to make us a forever thing,
admiring extravagant,
expensive dresses,
that dance in my head,
resting under my crowned tresses,
to the smooth sounds
of the jazz band I hear,
ever since we first kissed,
their floating fabric,
filled up with each...
ugh...
Don't get me started.

Lady,
they say that you're a criminal,
but I know you'll be the one,
locking me up,
waving keys in front of me,
as I lean across the bars
of this lovely love affair,
drunkenly singing of your sweetness to the air,
I'm not going anywhere,
now that I've been resurrected,
radioactive for your romance,
mutating,
finally growing a heart,
where before,
there had been an island of "if only I had a..."

Love,
you are the one thing I couldn't buy.
Not that I could afford anything,
in this store anyhow.

Staying After School

Valleys,
groves,
hills and fields,
my love,
I heard your name in every one,
every waning whisper of the wind,
as I lay in your lap,
wary but wild,
and you read to me.
I was taken from the ground,
a little girl lost to your gust.

I must stress,
I was literate before we met,
but under your passionate perception,
my eyes were carefully cut open,
extended,
immensely,
suddenly selfless,
I learned how to read,
with my humble, hungry hands.
You stripped me down,
building back up,
until I was taller than the trees,
where you taught me how to Polish kiss.

We built nature,
with paper,
after hours,

when the moon was moving closer.
My naked neck,
made for your hook.
A pretty lamb,
and a man who should have known better,
but was too beaten up by life to care.

I fell asleep on roses,
in your coral clasp,
one finger on your lips,
to shush the sheep,
so I wouldn't awake,
from our forest filled fantasy.
I don't suppose you ever loved me,
or, I, you,
or maybe we do,
still,
and we just pretend,
so the chasm we created,
doesn't feel so confining.

We Need To Talk About Onision

It is time,

for everyone,

with a camera,

to peel back,

the brown spotted,

yellow skin.

Bananas to blenders.

Boob squeezes.

Whatever.

Let's make a documentary!

So,

what if he's the monster,

that's been here all along?

Or maybe, that's that girl,

or me,

or you,

or the addition of stories,

in an attempt to mimic Instagram,

who was mimicking Snapchat in the first place,

in an attempt to bring us closer to the daily lives,

of people we cannot summon the bravery to direct
message.

"Eugenia Cooney: Let's Save Her."

Maybe,
I choose Onision,
because he reminds me of the one,
who tore off my skin,
until I was a baby in a blender,
leaving me,
spinning and screaming,
as he monologued,
about how it was easy to hate on him,
and how he was grateful,
for those that understood,
that he wasn't a bad guy.

"Rant! YouTube's Punching Bag, Onision. Double standards."

Maybe,
he was the Onision,
that's been here all along?
Maybe,

they are not the same,

but I heard my voice,

in a blue haired girl,

who refused remission in chains,

and tattoos,

so I followed the sound,

to the red and white lights,

and I drank,

and drank,

until I was deaf.

"*Fake cryers vs real crying (YouTubers)*"

Maybe,

the Onision,

the Character,

the Greg,

had been here all along,

but couldn't see,

the way people crowded around the red and white
blender,

shoving him inside,

for a smoothie of receipts and regrets,

that doesn't taste any good,

but feels very necessary.

Maybe he couldn't see,

until the première countdown was over,

until it was too late,

and he was dancing down their throats,

singing his banana ballad,

as they wipe their lips,

with dead presidents,

and sponsored T-Shirts.

"He's still out there. Be safe."

Boob Squeeze.

Buenas Noches

I hope you sleep well,
soothing,
smooth,
silk sheets,
just dream,
the world can wait,
love.

I have slept,
to the sound of your footsteps,
wishful white noise,
as my mind fills,
with dreams of us,
dancing on the dark side of the moon,
now,
it's your turn.

After Hours Alarm

You text me every night.
"You ok?"
But the way you move,
from my mood,
to your dick,
makes it so clear,
that you don't care how I am.

A Gun With Tomorrow On The Side

It rains.
It's raining once again.
She's never been bad,
but she never made good.
She's waiting for life to catch up,
and tell her it loves her.

Nothing changes,
no matter how hard she wishes,
and how long she waits,
but she's dreaming that maybe it could,
her eyes,
fluttering,
when sleeping,
when waking,
and it's primitive,
dissociative.

She's not sure there's any more.
She has a gun,
with tomorrow scratched on the side,
and a car,

that she stole.
She's blessed,
but she's broken,
on the shore,
remembering who she used to be,
making friends with the past,
kissing it's cheeks,
eyelids that flutter,
hair,
it's smile.

She tries to replicate it,
strapped down,
tied up in terror,
trying to wake up,
make the morning come,
and the sun,
smile at her again,
as she goes free,
listening to Journey,
in a gay bar,
and I love her,
but I have to leave her,
on a train,

going anywhere,
but where she is,
because I love her,
but I can't save her,
and I never could.

Taste

It's a shame,
that a darling as delicious as you,
has such drastically dreadful taste,
in the things you put,
inside the mouth that I miss.

I'm not sure,
if I'm referring to your taste in wine,
or your taste in women,
but I tried that wine,
and had to mute it with milkshake,
because,
no offence,
but it was fucking disgusting.

I'm shaking right now,
sharing my shame,
with my nosy notebooks,
who are desperate to hear,
how desperate I am for you to call.

I drank a bottle of your white wine,

'cause it reminded me of you...

Brandon Teena

Life tried to speak,
another existence,
decades of denial,
that decayed,
until he was standing,
saying his name,
under the starless sky,
hushed and hopeful,
that the world would echo back,
and suddenly,
the sky was so full of stars,
saying his name,
hushed and hopeful,
that he could hear them.

Love Of My Life

I promise,

you'll be the love of my life,

not just because I'm lonely,

and never learned how to like,

without tripping and tumbling into trouble,

too much from the very start,

but I promise,

you'll be the love of my life,

because each shade of you,

is a palette,

that the world has jumped into,

and I am so in awe,

of the art that you are,

and the way your turned the one drab world,

to a watercolour whirlpool of whimsy,

that I will stand and gaze,

for the rest of my life,

so there will be no time,

for me to meet another love of my life.

Unreliable Witnesses

Wrapped in trauma,
parcel of pain,
passed around the circle,
at a meeting of monsters,
who trade in candy and cash,
hiding their deadly deals in plain sight.

Lonely carnage carousel,
costing more every time it goes round,
a ride that lasts forever,
scarring and staying,
as police parade outside the gates,
with icy eyes,
that do not close,
but will not see.

I swear,
by almighty God,
that the evidence they shall give,
shall be the truth,
the whole truth,
and,

nothing but the truth,

but,

you have to want to believe them,

whether they are the perfect victim,

or not.

Life, Uh, Finds A Way

We played Jurassic Park,
in the arcade,
shooting at the Spinosaurus,
in silence,
with one hand each,
on our fraudulent firearms,
and the other,
exploring the empty space that existed between us.

We were just kids,
in a digital jungle,
running away from reality,
that had decided to dress as a T-Rex.
For a few minutes,
we were brave,
battling the beast of being in love,
with the wrong one,
at the wrong time.

Dinosaurs danced down the screen,
and we were alone,
pushing in another pound,
for another precious period in paradise,
where you are brave enough to be mine,
and maybe we will kiss,
during the brief moment the screen goes dark,
and the booth is barren of lights to snitch on us,
and maybe we will run away,
spending our prize tickets on fake passports,

and alcohol to numb the wounds we leave behind.

You told me that you weren't afraid,
taking my hand,
babying me,
to make yourself feel better,
but I felt your terrified fingers tremble,
as a triceratops trailed us,
and your phone began to vibrate on the dashboard,
as she called you.

Bathroom Lines

He used to take fifty four minutes in the bath,

giving concerts to the grubby tiles,

as I crossed my legs,

cursing the fact that I hadn't insisted on the second bathroom,

that was way out of our price range,

and now,

when I wake up,

to once again visit a world,

that carries on much the same as it would if I didn't,

I cross my legs,

for fifty four minutes,

mouthing his Morrissey and Lady GaGa set list to myself,

so it feels like he is still here.

The Romantic Adventures Of A Solemn Statue

I used to think I was stronger than tonight,

but being made of stone,

only lasts so long,

and the way life rains upon me is violent,

virtually unstoppable,

so,

isn't it natural that I cracked eventually?

Falling away from myself,

Crying,

so crazy,

remade in your rehabilitative embrace,

finding respite,

in gentle kisses,

that I know I'll regret,

when I awake,

stone again.

Girls In The Graveyard

You're mine,
when I settle my subconscious,
on soft pillows,
slipping into the chateau of sleep,
chasing you,
constantly thinking
about the fair features of your face.
I invite you to immerse yourself,
in freedom fantasies,
in which I can admit,
that night has fallen,
along with my inhibitions,
and I belong to you,
breaking my brain,
to try and understand,
how you broke inside me,
giving myself to you,
using my own hands.
Help yourself,
to my heart.

Don't Be A Bitch, I Just Want To Get To Know You

He said,

"Let's get some drinks",

a confusing cross between a question,

and an order.

I thought,

"Who the fuck does this stranger think he's talking to?"

but,

I whispered,

"Sorry, I have a boyfriend."

and ran home,

watching the scene,

over my shoulder,

to ensure I was alone.

Toast

I saw a woman on the bus,

who,

from behind,

was a very tempting twin of yours,

and as I tripped into the seat behind her,

which suddenly became lava,

I could think of nothing

but the way

you try to trick me into toast,

every morning,

by approaching the bed,

adorable in an apron,

ambushing me,

while I am too tired to resist.

Insomnia

Your hands were soft,
dainty and delicate,
lulling me,
late night lullabies,
crossing the clear borders,
I'd set out with the covers,
intimate invasions,
of my insecure insomnia,
that feels frightening,
until I am in your arms,
annexed but adored.

Please Be Gentle With The Gifts I Give You

She was so beautiful,
that I lost my mind.
I was obsessed,
possessed by her.
I kept her locked away,
in a secret place,
painted with poppies,
chained to a pink bed,
with handcuffs made of strawberry laces,
and I would sit on the sheets,
watching her,
as she stared back,
pleading to go outside.

I tried to resist,
knowing that once I freed her,
she was no longer mine,
but she was so beautiful,
and I knew that you would love her,
in the same insane way I did,
so,
one night,

I nuzzled into her chest,
and chewed at her chains.

I closed my eyes,
feeling her slip away,
into the night,
and I tried,
for twenty whole minutes,
to resist chasing after her.
I thought I'd chain myself to where she'd slept,
but my hands shook,
and my eyes streamed,
so,
I,
addicted as I knew I'd always been,
sought her out,
again.

I ran for twenty days,
in twenty minutes,
until I found her,
thoughts and judgements all across her,
crawling across every part of her body,
hands,

picking her apart,
like candy floss,
as she looked up at me,
the glee gone from her eyes,
as she realised,
she was better off inside my head,
where no one can criticise her.

Fulfilled

It wasn't until you left me empty,
that I learned how to overflow.
Suddenly,
in solitude,
I had everyone I needed.

When I Look At You

It should be noted,
that I'm lonely,
when I look at you.
Not only then,
it's not exclusive,
but you make me feel so...
(Nope)
Rhyming feelings with colours,
clicking clichés,
making myself sick,
of being infected with your affection,
my real selfish screaming,
all my tantrums,
internally yearning,
every time I look at you.

Sunday Best

You pull your cap down low,
hiding from the summer sun,
and all it has to say about the life you lead.
Your beat up Sunday best,
tells me all the places you've travelled,
to try and be the man you think I need you to be,
but you tell me,
with a sleepy arm slumped over my shoulder,
that you're just fine.

Fortune

My ace of cups,
I drank you up,
lounging on the soft ground,
carpet cuddling up to me,
as I gazed at the stars,
all my cards,
my painted nails were a wand,
and my mind was awash,
tapping on the side of the Titanic,
to see if it could echo back a message.

High Priestess,
the moon is hanging out,
asking me,
what this all means,
and I was wondering,
if you could spare some time,
from your busy schedule,
of monopolising my mind,
to give us a clue.

I Want You So Bad

I'll be waiting, as always,

wishing you wouldn't tease me with time,

all this wasted, waiting time,

nearing insanity,

taking breath after breath,

yearning for the moments I've earned,

opening my eyes real wide,

urging you to me,

smoking away my nerves,

observing the urgency and angst as my hands dance
in my pockets,

begging for your body as a partner,

as you finally arrive,

destroying my resolve.

I want you,
so bad.

Aimee

You looked so suspicious,
like those nonces,
caught by Dark Justice.
See,
the thing is,
I don't trust you,
troubled by the way I watch you,
not like a movie,
but late night CCTV,
troubled when you torture me,
being bold and beautiful,
cold but captivating,
keeping me guessing,
always stressing,
that I want you,
but I can't trust you.

Who is Aimee?
Why did you leave her on my desk,
every photo and text,
unlocked and unleashed,
in my peaceful play area,

where I go,

to try and take you from my thoughts,

but,

of course,

you couldn't stand it not being about you,

for one second,

so you sent her to harass me,

fucking Aimee,

on my desk,

with her perfect body,

and a kiss on the end of even the mundane messages.

Fucking Aimee,

fucking you,

while I fucking agonise over it.

Let's Be Real, This Is About Instagram

If you don't spy yourself,
on your daily scrolls,
through the endless screens,
of serene scenes,
don't worry,
darling.

If you enviously,
and endlessly stream a dream,
open mouthed laughter,
against a beautiful backdrop,
of a place you feel you'll never visit,
immaculate images,
flowing flower filled hair,
that glistens in the picture perfect sun,
know that you're not the only one.

Know that your life
is just as enchanting,
because,
to someone,
you are a serene scene,

and they can't imagine an image without you.

I'm Your Boyfriend Now, Nancy

It's midnight,
and I'm wearily awake,
because you are invading,
infringing on my dreams,
stalking me as I sleep.
You have a sweet smile,
as you do it,
we're in your car,
or under the pier,
and you are holding my hand,
like you're in love with me,
taking my lips,
with yours,
as if they mean the world to you,
and I am almost afraid to wake up,
addicted to the way I imagine us,
wishing you could frighten me,
like Freddy,
so I could run away,
and resist you.

Tonight,

I am awake.

I remain,

craving rest,

perched on the end of my bed,

drinking cup after cup,

of whatever it takes,

to keep you away,

because I know that when I see you,

I'll rip myself to pieces, if you ask me to.

December 1952

I am staring at the ceiling.
The eyes you loved,
don't blink tonight.
You wed your hands,
to the soft skin of my neck,
then carry me across the threshold,
to the living room.
You love me so deeply,
that I fall into the floor,
under the insulation,
taking all your secrets,
to my graceful grave.

You lay,
sometimes,
on the bare boards,
covered in my clothes,
asking the air for my perfume,
pleading in pathetic whispers,
for me to forgive you.

Pink, White, Red and A Kiss

Is it really so hard to do?
Am I incapable?
Maybe I could learn,
answering questions,
lying that I'm not afraid to ask them,
eyes unable to be honest,
staying closed and critical,
begging myself to hide behind the boys I knew.
Is it really so hard to do?
Am I incapable?
Nah, I'm honest, if you know acrostics.

Storyteller

London lights,
darling,
I swear you said,
you'd steal me away,
and we'd housesit the city,
hiding,
learning,
under lines of lovers,
from real life,
the police,
my pretty parents.
We were so sweet,
but I was just a little girl,
reading and needing,
and you were one hell of a story teller.

Tell me a story,
where everything is fine,
though I am a million miles from you,
now far too old for bedtime stories.
I am still crying and clawing at things to come,
clinging to tonight.

My pink nails and black hair turn white,
as you ask me,
"Where are you going, sweetheart?"

All I know,
is that I read your name,
with blind, beautiful eyes,
across a million different words,
that fill my head,
until I am a girl again,
at your desk,
handing my heart to you,
and your red pen.

Boyz 4 Now

I guess you're the guy,
I dreamed up,
just for summer,
something to do,
something to study,
something sturdy,
until I'm weak again,
adventurous,
annoying,
and a distant memory that you will occasionally text.

I'm learning to like you,
a little more every day.
I improv interest,
in the sports you like,
so I can see you excited somewhere
other than my bed.

I am quietly curious,
knowing enough to get by,
knowing goodbye comes,
at the moment when hello feels right.

Maybe it won't last for life,

in fact,

I'm counting on it,

because when the trees lose their leaves,

I've fall from your branches too,

to spend autumn,

telling the world all the things I miss most about you.

All You Need Is Smiles :)

You asked me to smile a little bit more,
so I skipped into the kitchen,
decorated in rainbow ribbons.
I hopped up onto the breakfast bar,
babbling about bubbles and boyfriends,
juggling nonsensical knives,
that could cut through your nerves,
as you stare,
in despair,
watching me drop all but one,
using the last,
to craft a sticky, sweet smile,
from the leftover jam.
:)

Lavender Love

Love Is like lavender,
you know,
it can send you to sweet
sleepy nights,
deep dreams,
where the darkness can not touch you,
but lavender love can swarm you,
overpowering the oxygen,
until you cannot stand it,
if you're not careful.

Narco Nights

I got out my best pen,
my shaking hands,
the same as your swivelling eyes.
I wrote you a letter,
and said I was leaving.
I knew you'd slur a reply.
I knew I'd stay.

I stared at my arms.
Perhaps they could end up like yours,
painted in polka dots,
tainted by tracks,
that I could never train for.
I could trade paracetamol,
for pethidine,
drowning in drink,
and be a daughter you finally recognised.

I made myself small,
kneeling at your chair,
summoning the day we met,
3:18PM,

held in your arms,
and a hospital blanket.
I begged in baby talk,
hoping you'd recall,
the times you knew how this all worked.

You didn't hear.
You didn't slur a reply.
You'd fallen asleep again.
Nuzzled into narco night nooses.
You didn't read my letter,
I didn't leave.
Neither did you.
I phoned for an ambulance.

Valentine's Day Dinner

I loved you,

love,

ignoring table manners,

at Il Padrino,

sitting with my lusty lips agape,

elegant elbows disgracing themselves,

on the table,

to take a peek,

at the way you seduced spaghetti,

charming it,

like a sordid snake,

from your fork,

to your pretty face.

The Cycle

In case you wondered,
this is another poem,
about a lonely life,
that I am unfortunately trapped in,
because it is easier
to write away my dismay,
than to talk to another person.

Don't Think About Her

I was lying in bed.

My hand was somewhere,

that I don't like to talk about.

I was thinking about men.

The only wet thing in my bed,

was my face,

as I wept,

knowing I couldn't think away the truth,

or the way I desperately wanted to think of her.

Wallpaper

You had come to help my mother move house.

We were pretending that you were just a friend,

because it's hard to explain the desperation of your separation,

when you're separating someone else's whole life apart,

to pack into neat boxes,

where nothing is complicated.

We said we'd save it for dinner,

we'd tell her about us over dinner,

a far away dinner,

that we don't have to think about,

so,

for now,

every now and then,

we'd sneak off.

You were a rushed but romantic whirlwind,

on my childhood bed.

A tender tornado

taking my mind off all the anxious thrill of moving on.

I was ignoring my ex,

in my pocket,

his texts,
jealous green,
ran up my screen,
across a picture of us,
that we had taken at Westminster Bridge,
where your hands had softly asked my waist
"Fuirich còmhla rium?"
and I understood
your hands were as sweet and sentimental
as the rest of you.

I wasn't sure why,
almost feeling envious of the way you could look at
me,
and see somebody you wanted to be close to.
It was that day,
on Westminster bridge,
where the wind seemed to pull us together,
giving your well spoken hands exciting ideas,
that I decided I would look at that picture every day,
keeping you on my screen,
so close,
that I could almost hear your soft whisper
every morning that I awoke without your hands,

and their exotic accent (well, it's exotic in Kent).

So,

all that being said,

you can imagine how annoying it became,

to see someone running up and down the happy
memories I was trying to make.

I couldn't even remember how his hands sounded,

and I certainly didn't care,

so I put my phone in my pocket,

pretending that we were in a place with no reception,

so I could be received by the safe span of your arms.

Gypsy Rose

Pills under my pretty tongue,
that never had a wrong word on it.
I promise,
I'll be a lovely living doll.
Mama,
will I always be a beautiful girl?
Will you always dress me with the list,
condition couture,
downloaded while I slept?
Could you tell me what's wrong with me today?
Tell me why I can't be like the girls I see?
Tell me why I can't explore summer skies,
Coca Cola nights?

Why am I,
tethered to the bed we share,
by a feeding tube,
and a list of conditional couture,
downloaded while I slept,
slipped into my life,
until my life,
is just your medical mood board,

and I am just your lovely living doll,
who never learned to live?
Mama,
will I always be a beautiful girl?

Getting Lost With You

I took you on a scenic route,
ten minutes across town,
that took forty three.
Forgive little old me,
for my inability to read a map,
or to read that look on your face,
that could say you are amused,
or irritated.

You kept asking me,
to ask for directions,
but I am deceptively shy,
an extravagant introvert,
who only ventures from her shell,
for a knock that only you can do,
and none of these strangers,
who may have directions,
know that particular incantation.

The secret was,
you knew,
all along,

that I was leading us,
up the garden path,
and off the planet,
(by innocent accident)
but you were too sweet on me,
the wide eyed way I wandered,
my silly smile at the ground,
as we arrived at yet another dead end,
that you couldn't stand to take the initiative.

So we walked,
aimlessly,
but happily,
pointing at street after street,
consulting a map I could not read,
because I failed geography,
and because my eyes were too busy,
with the scenic sweetheart beside me.

She Wore Black and White

I met my twin last night.
She wasn't my twin,
in the traditional sense,
but I remembered her face,
still so young,
unaware of the trouble to come.
I could place her,
at about sixteen,
in the summer before sixth,
shyly parading the planet,
in dresses that flowed like streams,
finally accepting that she was enough,
because a man told her she was,
with his mouth,
and a kind tone of voice,
in a way that most others couldn't manage.

I dreamed of her,
last night.
You know,
I told you,
about my weird dreams.

I've been seeing so many people,
from my past,
parading the planet,
as I retire to rest,
pulling at what's left of my mind,
to try and uncover
why I am suddenly so happy
to see the worst days of my life,
but now I know.

I'm so sure,
that I only let them explore me,
again,
in the way they invaded before,
because I hoped,
it would bring her out of hiding,
and we could escape,
to the farthest corners of my imagination,
so I could be alone,
with the girl I loved,
before the world tore her to pieces.

Everybody Has A Cult Leader, And I Guess You're Mine

I was sad all summer,

wailing in the warm night,

filling pages with my rages,

aching for him,

before he'd even gone.

Dear diary,

does he know what he does to me?

Singing snippets of songs about cinnamon,

by a jazz singer,

who describes him,

like she was caught in his cult too,

swallowing my pride and my dignity,

kneeling in defeat,

drinking from the neck of madness,

ageing and regressing,

at frightening, lightning speed.

My love's charismatic nature,

created and culled silent screaming operas,

silk gloves on,

love's gloves off,

I am tied up in ropes of my own making,

shaking,
pulling to be free,
knowing I will tie myself to him,
anyway.

Why, yes,
I would die for you,
darling.
Why do you ask?

St Pancras

We had been together six months,
when she asked me again,
to tell her about myself.
I thought about just handing her my press bio,
running from the room,
where I didn't have to confront my coldness,
and the way it blistered her beautiful skin.

Would it be such a sin,
to just go home,
put on a record,
and talk like lovers,
the old fashioned way?
With her graciously ignoring how I freeze up,
pushing her away,
when she gets too close,
not vocalising what she knows I'm holding back,
kissing in candlelight,
so she can't see the depressing depth of my scars.

I think about all the pages of my past,
that she might not be able to get past,

scrunched up in the back of my mind,

are the days I've said goodbye to,

cautiously replaced,

by carefully curated presentations,

pretty, perfect pictures,

that gloss over my less glorious days.

We are running for a train,

her and who I currently am,

I turn back,

and see old days and old ways chasing me.

I am thinking again,

about the press bio,

where I pushed away the way things were,

ushering in new beginnings,

where I could be someone she wouldn't feel
sympathy for,

or tread on tear stained eggshells to reach.

I think of each and every day before I met her,

trying to trust her enough,

to have the kind of heart I think she has,

driving myself mad,

pretending I was born,

at twenty four,
trying to Facetune my life,
until it is safe for her to see,
so she'll never know,
that my life overflowed so many times,
when I was too young,
and my hands were too small,
to reach out and reign it in.

I don't know where to begin,
and I'm conscious of keeping things light,
not dropping my whole deal on her dainty head,
because I can't even handle that,
though I've been built by all that I've been through,
and now we've missed the train,
I'm pooling the platform with the bruises life left,
and I can't catch my breath...

There's nothing left.
She's broken the walls,
stepping over the stones I placed around myself,
a spell,
to keep what's left of me safe,
an enchantment that screams

"Please, I've had enough."
but she is brave,
when I cannot be,
becoming my new spell,
breathtaking bricks,
built all around my messed up moat.
her arms speak so loud,
telling me that she has the kind of heart,
that I think she has,
and while the world walks past,
I am learning how to be loved gently.

Ol' Brown Eyes Is Back

When I was seventeen,

I decided,

much like Joanne,

that I was going to scam my way to being a
Caucasian woman.

Being biracial was cancelled,

'cause I had spent my EMA,

(god, that fucking ages me),

on white girl foundation,

and a relaxer kit,

that was on sale at Superdrug.

It was time,

to be the messiest,

most dramatic

Caucasian woman that my neighbourhood had EVER
seen.

I had also ordered an information pack,

from a darling doctor,

who promised to give me a perfectly petite nose.

Just a little internally racist razzle dazzle,

(can I be racist against myself? Asking for a friend),

and I could be like everyone else,

walking down the street,
without worrying about stop and search,
shopping sans security guard stalkers,
seeing myself on screens,
and magazines.

There was just one problem,
as there often is.
I could paint my previous identity,
until it was white and bright,
(**_YIKES_**),
and get my face bent into a whiter shape,
choking the life out of my hair with chemicals,
but,
I knew,
as soon as I surveyed my new face,
I'd be staring,
with the centre of sunflowers.

My Brown eyes.
My ol' brown eyes.
I couldn't bare to cover them with contacts,
for sentimental and squeamish reasons,
so,

I decided,

that being a white woman was simply too difficult,

(I have no idea how my mother does it)

and I'd spend my nose job money,

on sunflowers.

Filling my home,

with the beauty I finally saw,

in my eyes.

<u>Netflix and Nothing</u>

California love,
silver screen, to our open eyes.
We don't see real life.

Navigation

I got lost,
when you decided to find yourself.
Fucking off,
where my eyes couldn't explore,
while my friends find me,
joining hands,
circling the scene,
skipping around my screams,
chanting like school children.

Fuck boys.
It's okay,
You don't need him anyway.

I am streaming,
messy scrawls fall from my face,
swimming all around me,
and I drink my darkness,
knowing that my theatrical friends are lying.

<u>Tears In Lost Property</u>

When I walked away from you,

I turned to God,

settled in her arms,

to wait,

with tearful eyes,

lips that could only talk about my mistakes,

and why it's all so hard.

I told you I would hurt you,

so I'd feel secure,

that you wouldn't dare do that to me,

but you did,

and now I'm not sure if my tears belong to you,

or my ego.

Yet Another Dig At The WeLo Queens. Cool Story, Bro.

I once heard someone say,

with a fairly fraudulent fancy accent,

as she placed yet another business card that I didn't ask for,

into the pocket of a dress that she insisted was "the most absolute, gorgeous thing",

that if you're a nice person,

you don't need to tell someone repeatedly,

how nice you are.

"I just feel like people should always be,

like,

super authentic,

you know?"

Now,

I never said I was authentic,

you know?

I'm a fake fucking fantasy,

like those summer blockbusters,

based on true events,

and sexed up,

by some smug twat with a pen,

and a basic knowledge of marketing,

but she is.

Do you know how I know,

dear reader?

She keeps telling me.

It is all she can apparently say.

I didn't realise that there were this many ways to insist on one's authenticity.

I only came over to this side of the room to get to the toilet.

I really need a wee.

Fuck's sake.

She won't stop fucking talking.

Anyway,

she went on to say,

with great flair and theatrics,

that nobody was really watching,

"Darling,

I just always try to be real,

you know?

Authentic."

Well,

sis,

I'm afraid I've got some bad news,

for the super authentic angels,

who insist on telling people,

who really don't care,

repeatedly,

how authentic they are,

to make up for a lack of personality.

Anyway,

a dress with pockets,

huh?

Now,

THAT,

is some authentic brilliance.

Royal Borough of Kensington and Chelsea

Generic, grimy grey,
crawling across the sanctuary,
of people who are doing the best they can,
with what they can.
Old ladies,
struggling up stairs for centuries,
passing kids who peer through balcony bars,
kids who never quite clicked,
that they didn't get the same start.

There is a nervous energy in the walls,
floor to roof,
violent negligence chasing screams
up the cladding,
and I remember the maisonette of my youth,
maturing with my mother,
not quite clicking,
that most homes don't have holes in the walls,
for me to hide my hopes and dreams.

Now I am tall,
putting my hopes and dreams into the air,

no longer hidden in holes in the wall,
I am nervous when I see tower blocks,
because they contain lives,
as precious as those outside,
but the country never quite clicks,
that they aren't built to protect them.

Honeymoon

I miss missing you.
Acting so alien,
when I stare at our story,
trying to take back the moment I unchained my heart,
and set it free.
Maybe,
someday,
I'll leap back in love with you again,
hanging out in our honeymoon hours,
as it was.

Oh,
you know,
it's hard to accept,
that my heart is mine again,
when I spent so long,
telling her she belonged to you.

Siren Sailor

I leapt into your legs,
making them saunter off a cliff,
into the unsuspecting sea,
so you could be at peace,
with the wailing waves,
and out of my head,
far away,
where I could not reach.

I bathed in my bed,
drowning in a drought of you,
crying out things I didn't know I still felt,
grieving for the girl I was,
before I met you.
Halloween merged with Easter,
when you sprang up from deceitful death,
and I had to accept,
that perhaps it would be better,
to discuss the depths of my despair,
instead of imagining a time in which it didn't exist.

You crawled up the cliff,

with a seaweed crown atop your head,

rising like the messiah.

I could feel you,

reaching under my skin,

before you'd even reached my door.

It was easier,

when I could imagine you'd gone,

to a place I could not follow,

but now,

I'm confronted by you,

dropping by to wish me well,

when I wished you dead,

so it would hurt less,

to accept I couldn't have you.

The Night Was Divine

The night was divine,
the sun desperately clinging to the sky,
to catch a glimpse of us,
especially you,
a violet vision,
violently beautiful,
the king of hearts.

Finally,
my life had started.
I awoke from the banishment of my beginning,
rubbing my enchanted eyes,
until they were free of twenty two tears,
and I stared,
and I smiled,
on our hella,
bella notte.

Finally,
I could see beauty and joy,
in forgotten Tsingtao cans,
who could,

and would learn to love the lips of another.

Dancing ash,
abandoned on the ground,
but still streaming across the street,
as if anything was possible.
You reached out your hand,
which I stole,
hoping for your heart,
in time,
and the night,
my love,
was divine,
my love.
The night was simply divine.

I Saw My Psychic Today

I saw my psychic today.
I discovered
that you're still stalking me,
living in my hands,
my nightmares.

I tell myself,
screaming in an empty, echoing room,
that I don't care,
because I'm strong and stable,
prime minister of my own palace of reality,
but you invade,
no matter how many times I paint
empowering enchantments on the doors.

Thank U, Next!
I Will Survive!
I'm A Survivor!

No,
I'm not.
I barely made it out alive,

and I lock myself inside my house,

with my head,

seasoned with sand,

in the oven,

hiding with the rest of me,

from the big bad wolf,

who never bothers to knock,

and always drags his axe across my shelves,

beating and bastardising the beautiful books,

where I told my tales,

of how I was free.

He drags his axe,

like a serial killer,

from my kooky collection of horror movies,

that I watch daily,

just to see if I can find anything that chills my chest,

quite as much as him.

He drags his axe,

and the scrape is deafening,

before he swings back in,

saying,

"I'm sorry about before."

Sweetness

When I think of you,

I am blinded by July.

I am surrounded by the summer,

when all I did was adore you,

sitting on the beach,

throwing honey and hope to the sea,

listening to the same sixteen silly love songs,

imagining that our romance had possessed the world
around us.

Butterflies Only Live So Long

The passion that you had,
was your downfall,
all your dreams dangled you,
from your dainty, saintly ankles,
over pretentious piranhas,
tugging at the threads of your tragic tapestry.

You say the way you were was decayed,
but I still see it,
in the right light,
but,
butterflies only live so long,
my love.
Maybe it's your time.

Handwriting

I always hated parent's evening,
when a bunch of middle class people,
who had their lives together,
looked down their knowledgeable noses,
at me and my mum,
glaring,
as if we had dragged them,
from their cozy classrooms,
to our big, scary council estate casa.

They always told me that I needed to take pride in my
work,
as if a teenage egomaniac wasn't proud of her work,
what they really meant was that I needed to improve
my handwringing.
Wait.
That's not it.
Handwashing?
No.
Got it.
It says handwriting.
But you never said that to me,
because you understood what was beneath the

scribbled secrets.

Boys Who Like Playing With Cats

There are four years between us,
but you remark that some days,
(which feel like months),
it feels like four hundred,
as you lay,
four inches from me,
in a single bed,
containing two singles,
stupidly supposing that nothing suspicious will occur.

I am listening to subliminals,
through earphones,
turned down low,
so I can hear all the effort you go to,
to pretend you're asleep,
as you explore me,
and I feel like a fraud,
because I spent all day telling the walls,
carpets,
windows and washing machine,
that it isn't weird for you to be here,
because you're like a brother to me.

Some say,

that much like riding a bike,

you never forget how to...

Well,

as you may know,

I never learned to safely ride a bike,

but according to an anecdote you shared,

with the one who was merely a world apart,

many worlds ago,

that you then shared with me,

after sharing my bed,

and sharing a cigarette,

I am surprisingly proficient,

for someone with no balance,

no dexterity,

and no hand, eye coordination.

The Sun

We all share the sun,
but we can't learn
to share the ground,
that the sun lovingly looks at,
as she watches us play fighting,
with missiles,
and metal fences.

Please Papi

You pushed me to build a life,
and then you ruined it.
You don't even see it.
I display my dismay,
through drunken outbursts,
watching you,
through every screen I can see,
unsure of why you are still so unaware.

You used to be my heart's sugar daddy,
spoiling me,
until you got sick of it.
Then off you want,
and I was left,
a mansion full of meaningless memories,
deafening silence,
on a loop,
as I watch you ignore me again.

I keep expecting you to give me what I want,
because you always did,
until you didn't.

I'll keep screaming,
crying,
throwing the world against the wall,
until I am left with smashed,
broken,
nothingness.

<u>Mirror Image</u>

I loved her so much,

that when I looked in the mirror,

after she left,

the girl who left,

was staring back at me,

and so I chased her down,

in the high heels she always wore,

hearing her voice calling out,

into the empty evening,

and begged for myself back.

I'm The Princesa Of PortAventura

I heard a man say once,
that his heart was in the East,
with him at the edge of the West.
I felt the tension in his chest,
that gnawing, aching anguish,
when you know,
that your soul,
has been split in two,
one half resting with you,
but clinging to the slowly
slipping
fingers of its other half.

I didn't even know him.
I didn't even actually hear him.
I just read his pain,
on a twitter thread,
and I realised,
that my soul had split too,
a long time ago,
in a beautiful town,
as dry as a bone,

that sends chills through each of mine,
when I stop to picture her,
in my busy brain.

Yes,
my heart is stuck in a laborious loop,
reliving the eleventh of September,
and St John's Eve,
over and over,
wrapping our hands,
and our hopes,
to the days,
when the sun shone for me,
because I was Catalonia's daughter.

Don't you know?
I'm the Princesa of PortAventura,
all I taste is pleasure,
when I eat with my eyes closed.
I avoid all armadas,
that come to claim me,
because I am the darling of the sea,
hiding under the roaring waves,
that are rainbows in the bright sunshine,

and as I heard a man once say to me,
I can never be captured.

If I never open my eyes again,
bidding goodbye,
to clear beaches,
red and yellow skies,
then eventually,
my soul will wrap all around me,
tripping me up,
taking me home,
where I belong.

Bad Girls

I used to love dogs,

until I met them across barb wire badlands,

and I loved to sleep all day,

until it was all that I could do,

but now,

I'm so tired of napping my way out of boredom.

Blue used to be my favourite colour,

until it was all that I could see.

Pale blue walls,

sterile and senile.

They don't remember,

my regrets,

the secrets I tell.

I tell them again,

every day,

every minute,

as I sing to the night,

of my nightmares and nice thoughts,

for a future I forget I can't have,

because I'm surfing in a cycle,

that never ends,

and I will always be barred,

even when I'm free.

Comcast

The night and I,
invade your window,
impatient,
when you are so irresistible,
irresponsibly beautiful.
I waited for you,
as long as I could,
the night and I,
adorning Ardenlee,
until the pavement knew our footprint.

I looked down,
at my own perpetual path,
so I couldn't see the way you leant on the window
frame,
watching over your wayward baby,
wrapping my head in blossoms and fruit,
that fell from the forest around me,
so I couldn't hear your siren call.
You are the whole world,
exploding all around me,
your arms are a soothing supernova.

I may be dead.

I may yet die.

I may not ever understand,

but in your grasp,

I am free.

Buzzfeed Me Zaddy

Sometimes,

Buzzfeed promises to show me something,

that they say is making millennials lose their avocado
obsessed minds,

and I laugh,

because we're only renting them anyway,

at great expense,

so what do we have to lose?

She's Waking Up

When I was twenty six,
I tore my own heart,
beating and bleeding,
broken,
from my chest,
though she was quite comfortable,
and therefore inconvenienced,
by my insistence,
that we were fucking done,
professionally,
with the showmance of romance.

When I was twenty seven,
I met you,
and I crammed her back inside,
hoping your electric eyes,
could make her start again,
after a long sleep,
filled with nice nightmares,
of all the mistakes we had made before.

Pon Farr

We stayed up all night,
as my voice filled your body with blood.
Concentrated on corruption,
that we both knew you were wanting,
we felt out a constellation,
I tasted trouble on my tongue,
as you took me in your arms.

Give me hope,
give me heaven,
give me something to regret,
and to remember,
kiss my lips,
make me surrender,
help me sleep,
then wake me up again.

Did you think of me under these sheets?
I say your name,
until it loses all meaning,
and becomes a silly little song,
that repeats from the lips you relentlessly kiss,

high and sweet.

Hit By A Charming Train

I used to wait,

at Walthamstow Central,

for you to remember me,

because I,

in the great tradition of telenovelas,

had amnesia,

for the flourishing flower I was,

before I was hit by a charming train.

You were overseas,

I was overboard,

bored of being beholden to you,

but unable to get the courage,

to claim myself from your abandoned belongings.

I scribbled promises of a new life,

over your name,

that lay,

defiant,

across my skin,

knowing I could never escape,

the tracks I was tied to.

Sincerely, Jennifer x

He sends me intimate letters,
filled with thinly veiled issues.
Tells me tales of all the ways he failed,
to find happiness,
on the path he chose,
trying to be joyful,
but he's hateful and ungrateful,
until everything around him warps,
his whole world taking on his barren way of being,
until he's wandering through clouds,
of chaotic isolation,
seeing the world in black and white.

I am,
apparently,
a lighter shade of grey,
almost verging on colour,
if I hold him right,
or stay on the phone as he falls asleep.
He says I remind him,
of this bold but cold broad,
that saw potential in him,

once upon a time,
and he believes I'm made of madness and magic,
that can fix him.

He asks me,
if I love him sincerely,
every single time he writes,
and I reply,
with the same,
wry,
"Sincerely is how I end my letters,
but never how I live my life."
Hoping he will never know,
that I have wallpapered my room,
in his words.

If he wants me mad,
magic,
bold and cold,
then I will icily exist,
freezing out his panic,
with frosty fingertips,
enchanting him every night,
until we are both mad,

and glad to be stuck inside,
avoiding the sleet I have successfully conjured,
to keep him close.

I will never let him know,
that I felt warm,
sane,
human and changed,
for the very first time,
when he wrote to me,
with such tenderness.

Weird Dreams

I've been having a lot of weird dreams,
lately.
Baby,
maybe it's a sign,
that I can't read yet.

Or,
maybe I'm living another life,
in another sky,
that I can only see,
when I close my eyes?

But,
anyway,
when I'm there,
wandering through weirdness,
I am happy,
at least.
I always wake up,
nostalgic for the smile I wore,
the night before,
in my dreams.

Hotline To Heaven

Last night,
I lay alone,
dialling a hotline to heaven,
over and over,
referring to God as "Daddy",
and seeing lightning from the window,
growing dangerously close,
as he rolled his eyes,
hanging up,
until I called back up,
clutching my pearls,
as my teddy bear shook his head.

I whispered to God,
real breathy and babyish,
because after all,
maybe,
he's just a man,
and maybe he'll play along,
like the others do.
I whispered to God,
real tearful and terrified.

"Daddy, why did you make my heart so big,
if you didn't intend anyone to want a piece,
when they come round to play?"

Stick To Your Colouring Books, Dickhead

These boys,
posting parchment on the 'gram,
trying to teach girls how to behave,
calling out for some class,
but talking like they never graduated.

Crying about how every girl,
wants to be Kylie Jenner.
Crying about how girls won't cover up,
and by cover up,
they mean shut up.

These boys,
posting parchment on the 'gram,
say they want a girl,
with a mind like Jane Austen,
but the problem is,
they act like Giles Coren.

None of these women
asked for your misogynistic musings,
mate,

puking insecure, incel phrases,

onto parchment,

for the 'gram,

is not a talent.

Let Me Be Your Drug, Darling

Darling,

what have you done?

I have no right to,

but,

I wish you got high less.

You took a gamble with the guy I loved,

sending him round the roulette wheel,

ribs and pretty face,

broken by the blades of your bad habits,

while I sit on your steps,

smoking all your cigarettes,

singing sad songs to the moon.

Darling,

just out of the way,

where I can pretend,

that I can't see you unravelling,

revealing all the ways I wounded you,

before running away,

to pour alcohol and anxiety into my own war trophies,

won in battles,

that I lost,

far before our time.

Darling,
I wish I could drink less,
and ignore you more,
but when I am narcotic,
I am nostalgic for you.
My disgruntled daddy,
Blake, Sid, Clyde, Romeo,
I am a glamorous groupie,
criminal chanteuse,
dying to die with you,
because living apart feels too hard.

Darling,
when the morning comes,
my ballads replaced by birds,
who believe in the sunrise,
I hope you'll be alive,
to understand,
that I am overstating my intentions,
and affections.
When I loved you,
I was just a girl.

I don't know how to love you

like a grown up,

yet.

Sleep Paralysis Paradise

I crawl down the walls,

humming your favourite song,

all through the night,

threatening lullaby,

every time you try to sleep.

You expected me,

obviously,

unless I'm supposed to believe you're all dressed up
for no reason.

Restrain yourself, or I'll do it for you.

What are you dreaming about?

Is it me?

Free yourself,

exist with me.

Dead Doll

When I love someone,
I want them to be overwhelmed
with joy.
I want them to know nothing,
but the most exquisite enjoyment,
and that's how I knew you never loved me,
because you could never allow me to feel the same.

Cranfield Ward

He never said what he actually did.
Keeping the truth,
tightly under his tongue,
where he hides his pills,
before rolling them round to his cheek.
He says,
"There's nothing wrong with me."

He never got to know the outside world.
Patiently pacing,
as he plays the perfect patient,
until the truth is loose,
melting into his mouth.
He says,
"Why won't they let me out?"

He never told me his real name.
Chemicals kept him from me,
banging his back against the door,
to write a song,
about his medicated map to being trapped.
He says,

"Tell them not to let me go."

Penge East to Bickley

We sold everything we could see,
surviving the summer,
on pirated pro wrestling,
payday prosperity,
and sneaked cigarettes at Penge East station.

You'd ask if the barriers were open,
and I was never sure,
if you meant at the station,
or inside of me,
because you were the only one I trusted,
but I still had to keep you locked outside,
when we arrived,
passing me food and feelings,
through the living room window,
before you caught the night bus home.

I'm sorry that I never texted you back.

I Am Uncharted Territory, And She Is Wearing An Explorer's Hat

I am a sea of screaming sheets,

pledging allegiance,

pressing play,

on your intimate instruction tape,

the sounds celebrate,

as they parade across my conquered land,

laid out for you,

your new country,

of which you will be King,

Queen,

President and resident.

I leave my taxes

all across the floor,

a bomb site of silk and satin,

because it's laundry day tomorrow,

but tonight,

I am busy,

being educated,

and explored.

Lambs Who Live With The Stars

You were the last day of Cancer,
a sweet, sinful summer child.
The only pure thing about you,
was the blinding white shirt,
that kept your chest a prisoner,
pressed every morning,
the way your mother showed you,
an optical illusion
that runs through my mind all day,
the way I run after you,
time after time.

More and more desperate and delusional,
despite the way you warned me,
stroking my cheeks as I slept,
with tears in your eyes,
begging me not to love you,
because there can be good in you.
I know you don't want to see it,
having already made up your mind,
that you don't mind being so beastly,
but your eyes are not mine,

even though mine long for yours,
and my mind isn't quite made up about you yet.

You said you loved my hair high,
like all your other ladies,
because you loved to look at our faces.
You said you had good taste,
always choosing the best,
bringing all the brightest stars into your orbit,
because you were a sweet, selfish summer child,
and,
well,
I guess I am just another bright,
blinkered bulb in your observatory,
and maybe that's fine.
Maybe you had to keep all the lights on,
softly buzzing in the background,
of all your bad dreams,
because you thought you were full of darkness,
and maybe that's fine too,
but darling,
won't you think of the environment?

It's 3:18, and I Have Been Reborn

It's 3:18,

and I have been reborn.

The absolute state of this

is a miracle,

at last,

and I,

gleam,

tears streaming,

without a slap,

as I fall from the stars,

an absolute statement,

of smiling scars,

breathing,

and breathing,

and breathing.

It's 3:18,

and I am reborn.

Everything the world has shot at me,

is crumpled around my crib,

and when I grow up,

I'll paint it a pretty colour,

and I will wear my weariness as armour,
as I step into another war.
My bullet holes are so beautiful,
in the pale moonlight.

Some Things Are Worth Waiting For (Some Things Are Not)

He kissed my wrists,

and I felt like a princess.

He undressed each insecurity,

pouring praise.

I prayed,

it would never end.

I fell from Heaven,

enjoying attention,

adoration.

I was supernatural,

that night,

so close,

to somewhere I had never been,

guided from my guilt,

to a place of promised passion.

Then.

You like that, don't you?

Suddenly.

Tell me you like it, slut.

I was lost.

Say you like it, you slut!

Laying in the dark,
choking on betrayal,
my eyes wide,
my once kissed wrists,
horrified,
terrified,
like the girls he had seen,
consumed,
in HD quality.

My
tears
ran,
in
fear,
from what he had become,
and I, too,
was consumed,

torn to pieces by his once gentle hands,
that gripped my throat.

My screams,
drowned out,
by the cheers of his imaginary audience,
and the sound of him,
in a voice I once loved,
calling me a slut.

My Man Is Many Things

My darling,
you were once roses,
that I knelt beside,
with eyes full of tears,
wrapped in the rain,
that you later became,
falling around our hotel,
as we watched a bad JLo movie,
and I watched you,
with wide eyes,
remembering the time you were the ocean.

I drowned in you,
ocean angel,
determined to never learn to swim,
holding hands with humpback whales,
saluting the sailor you'd later become,
as I sank to the sound of your voice,
telling my marvellous marine mates,
about the time you were the sky.

I gazed up every second,

growing possessive,

knowing you could never be mine,

when you surrounded every part of the planet,

and though I loved to look,

at you looking down at me,

It would be easier to keep you all to myself,

if you were just a man.

My man.

Again

Because I could not stop,
I lost you.
I found a way to find you,
but I lost you,
again.
The search begins,
again,
again.

I could have brushed the evil
from your hands,
made you tea,
peppermint.
Sit with you,
as you talk to me,
about the band you used to play in,
old covers,
that nobody,
in any bar you bothered
wanted to hear.
You didn't ask about me,
again.

You only talk about you,

again.

I'm wondering why I came back,

again.

Again,

again,

again.

Grey Girl

There are glimpses of gold,
in the silver I sift through,
soft tresses,
caress me,
as they escape my curious fingers,
on their way to explore my essence,
you shape my shakes,
removing your glasses.
You kiss me,
and I am a river.

Welp

You're a realisation,
that I ignore,
because reality bores me to tears,
and I do enough crying,
anyway,
because I'm dramatic
(perhaps that's why you love me?)

Anyway,
you're a fucking disaster,
and you mess with my head,
but you're still a simple story,
straightforward,
a portrait of an artist,
that thought they were clever.

Your story has no message,
and it's messy,
(You told me you love me)
you have nothing to tell me,
but I am wide awake,
listening just in case.

I'm anticipating curiosity,

and bewilderment,

but right now,

I'm just waiting,

with much captivation,

and adoring awe,

because you,

yes,

you,

just told me you love me,

and I don't know how to deal with that.

Ah,

fuck,

I can't believe you've done this.

The People's Princess Of My Heart

You are to me,
what Princess Diana is,
to the Daily Express.
If I could,
I'd stand in newsagents,
showing shocked shoppers,
all the way your majesty manifests,
making sure they never forget,
that some of us,
were lucky enough,
to share the planet with you,
for a few brief moments.

I would pull them close to the paper rack,
insisting,
to the point of incoherence,
that you were the very essence of elegance.
Insisting that I didn't cry alone,
when you said goodbye,
because the world stood,
weeping with me,
as I dried all our tears,

with a handkerchief,
embroidered with your image,
my hands wet with ink,
and my loneliness.

I,
like the Daily Express,
am not known to exaggerate.
I promise.

<u>Reviews</u>

I wrote a beautiful book,

about how I loved her,

and how she left,

along with my mind,

and my will to live,

so,

naturally,

my inbox is full of dick pics.

Starlight

We've been to the ends of the earth,
my love,
and the heights of heaven,
have welcomed us,
when our faces were fused,
and we spoke only in sighs and screams.
We have sailed in the skies,
sunk lower than the ocean's depths.

We have done life to death,
my love,
but still,
you scold me,
for being so final,
so young,
and so,
I sit in your lap.
I remind your body, your mind,
my love,
that when you looked to the sky,
to wish for me,
I was the brightest star,

your sapphire gaze had ever seen,

and bright stars,

burn fast,

so lovely,

and lonely.

You sigh,

my love,

you scream again,

and then,

with faces fused,

we weep,

as I turn to ash,

in your learned hands,

so loved,

yet,

so lonely.

Watch the skies,

my love,

for I have grown brighter,

under your care,

and I want to say hello.

Collaboration

We both have the same cycle around the sun.
Twenty four hours,
doesn't mean more to me,
but,
still,
you stop,
brakes on,
standing before me,
as I try to get past,
and I sigh,
again,
because this happens every time.

You shake your head,
holding up your loneliness,
with a smile full of misplaced pride.
I just wanted to cycle past,
sharing some thoughts,
maybe gluing glory together,
but you had to make it something it wasn't,
because I'm expected to be professional,
but not too harsh,

gentle,

but respectable,

open to your unsolicited flirting,

but absolutely not a slut.

I often wonder,

as I take the bus,

because cycling became too much trouble,

why I didn't just pretend to be a man in the first place.

Wrapped Up Love

I am ice,
sometimes.
You try to break me,
with your pun filled pick axe,
but I'm just no fun,
sometimes.

I am trying,
most times,
to thaw as you thrill me,
while I hide glacial glee,
because I'm afraid of the frost,
I always feel,
when I venture too far outside,
without a winter coat,
each button,
full of wisdom,
from the cold snaps,
back to reality,
that I have weathered.

I will cry,

sometimes,
but my tears will make intriguing icicles,
for us to hang on a Christmas tree,
if you can endure my snow storm.

Maybe I could change for you...

The Good Life

I don't want to stop loving you,
because I don't know how to do anything else.
I know I did before,
there were others,
but this conversation is new,
because,
while I don't mean to sound clichéd and insincere,
I've never loved anyone,
the way I love you.
(Vomit emoji)
How could I?

You didn't do anything wrong,
I just love with such lustre,
listing every lovely like,
leaving the dislike column lonely,
because I swear,
I will adore every artefact,
in my carefully curated museum of muse,
because my eyes are secretly just rosy, regrettable
hearts.

All that said,

I can feel it.

I feel myself boiling bright red,

when you leave me on read,

tortured,

toiling and tearing at my lists,

my hand hovering,

armed with a pen,

over that dislike column.

I feel a chill,

when you touch me,

after leaving the toilet seat up,

for the hundredth time,

and I,

along with my icy fingers,

storm out of the bathroom,

after slamming it down,

and then I am a whirlwind of Baltic breezes,

and hurried,

flurried tears,

alone in my study,

because I didn't realise it would be this hard.

You didn't do anything wrong,

not really,

but I'm irrational and unrealistic,

because I thought love would always be perfect.

Off the page,

you're still exactly as I delicately and desperately
described you,

but you've grabbed one of my pens,

started adding your own ad libs,

and this whole thing,

is a cyclone of scribbles,

and screaming,

and,

as it all turns out,

when it comes to imagining the perfect person,

team work does NOT make the dream work.

I don't want to stop loving you,

because I don't know how to do anything else.

So,

I suppose I should close the books,

close my eyes,

and learn to love you,

as you are,

instead of how I imagined you.

Eight Twenty One. Baby, I'm In Love

I'm the casino queen,
who never made it out of the arcade,
smoking out on the street,
with your big eyes all across me.

I feel your hands on my waist,
your lust on my lips,
we share my last cigarette,
slinking back inside,
to avoid the storm.

Spending all our money,
on the slots,
lost in the lavish lights,
on rain soaked nights,
feeling like royalty,
because we're minimum wage millionaires.
Maybe we'll get lucky,
and win enough get Nando's for tea.

Necklace

I'm happy now,
swinging from the sky,
like a little child.
I hope you'll remember me,
with magic in my eyes,
spinning in the vibrant vines,
singing songs about winter,
as the summer sun swims through the window,
sleeping at my silent shoes.

I'm beautifully blissful,
blowing kisses to my soul,
as she sits on the end of the bed,
watching me swinging and shining,
the world crashing and crowding around me,
to get a better view.
I hope you won't be upset,
that I took the only thing I felt was still mine.

I wanted to be worthy.
It's my life,
and I can waste it if I want to.

Tell me,

could you ever get through to me?

I never wanted to be difficult.

I never wanted to be that girl,

who realised that she was loved,

too late,

as she watched from the window,

seeing her mother scream and shake,

at the terrible choice she made,

when selecting a necklace to wear for her last day on Earth.

Let's celebrate,

while we still have time,

while all that is just a dream,

while I am still firmly on the floor,

ignored by the light at the end of a tunnel,

that remains boarded up,

because it isn't my time.

Today,

I'll take a chance,

and be grateful that I couldn't find a necklace,

that matched my earrings.

Obituary

She is not dead,
you know,
irreverent,
irreversible ink,
seeped from her soul,
to places she had never dared explore.
She is in the days she dreamed of,
jaunting through jungles,
haunting the hills of Peruvian villages,
breaking into Buckingham Palace,
catching a ride on the sky,
down to the waves of the world,
because she spoke,
and she sang,
and she cried,
and she breathed,
and she existed,
so,
she will never end.

Hi,

Thank you so much for reading my book, I hope you enjoyed it! If you enjoyed reading my book, please feel free to visit my website, JenniferJuan.com to find lots of free to read content, as well as free to access video and audio content that you may also enjoy.

Besos, J x

About The Author

Jennifer Juan is a cultural melting pot of an artist. She is a writer, a musician, a producer, a film maker and a podcast host, currently residing in the Kent countryside, but dreaming of the ocean. A tornado of darkness and delicacy, Juan creates engaging and powerful projects, using a variety of mediums and platforms, each dripping with her signature playful, yet powerful style of writing.

Beginning her journey as an artist as a teenager, Juan graduated from The University of Greenwich in 2013, and began sharing her work on her personal website, JenniferJuan.Com, as well as through social media, posting written poetry and video projects.

In 2017, Juan began producing a weekly podcast, Sincerely, Jennifer x, sharing her poetry and insights into her writing techniques, and also released several printed volumes of poetry, including the critically acclaimed "Home Wrecker", and in 2018's "27, With A White Lighter" as well as her debut EP, "Wildflowers", with her music gaining over 29,000 listeners on Spotify alone in her first year as a recording artist.

Acknowledgements

Thank you to all my readers, the listeners of my podcast, the visitors of my website, and my subscribers on YouTube, for supporting my work, and for allowing me to do what I love and share it with you.

Thank you to my family and friends for always being so supportive and loving. Thank you so much Mum, Grandma, Grandad, Keiron and Lauren, I love you.

Thank you to my dear friend Amanda, for her never ending support and love.

Thank you my hazel honey for your love, for the joy you give me, and for the ideas you inspire, just by being you.

I love you AB. You saved me from drowning.

Thank you AJ for being an inspiration, and being unapologetically you.

Thank you CT, for reminding me that I am still alive, even if you cannot bear to read this book, and find out all that I've been up to...

Thank you to Carmina and all the great team at She Grrrowls for being so supportive and being my favourite place to perform.

Thank you to the people I met, on the way to where I

am now, for all the ways you have found your way to me, and inevitably, into my work, with particular thanks to the ones who taught me so many things, the ones who helped me forget everything I had learned, the ones I have many happy memories of, as well as the ones I don't, and, of course, and the one I have been walking towards my whole life, without realising, because my internal sat nav doesn't work, and I cannot read maps.

1087 days, mi alma, and then we will finally be free.

X

Connect With Me

Follow me on Twitter: @MissJSquared

Follow me on instagram: @MissJSquared

Check out my podcast: Sincerely, Jennifer x

Friend me on Facebook:
https://www.facebook.com/missjsquared/
Subscribe to my blog: JenniferJuan.com